Introduction

Pete Rose learned to be a fearless, aggressive baseball player from his father, who was a semipro athlete in Cincinnati. Pete always loved baseball and, as soon as he had graduated from high school, was signed up by his beloved hometown team—the Cincinnati Reds.

Since then Pete has excelled as a third baseman, while proving his versatility by playing second base, left field and right field as well. Today he is the captain of the team and one of the highest-paid players in baseball with a remarkable record of seven 200-hit seasons and a lifetime batting average of well over .300.

This is the story of Pete Rose, whose boundless energy, hard work, and skill helped lead the Cincinnati Reds to victory in the 1975 World Series, bringing them their first championship in thirty-five years.

Sports Hero
PETE ROSE

by Marshall Burchard

G. P. Putnam's Sons • New York

PHOTO CREDITS

Courtesy of:

Cincinnati Reds, pp. 12, 13, 24, 34, 46, 56, 86

Bruce Curtis, pp. 49, 75, 82

Peter Travers, pp. 2, 94

UPI, pp. 9, 26, 28, 30, 37, 38, 41, 43, 44
50, 60-61, 63, 66, 68, 71, 77, 84, 91

Western Hills High School, pp. 6, 16, 22

Wide World, pp. 54, 72, 78, 79, 92

PRINTED IN THE UNITED STATES OF AMERICA
07210
Library of Congress Cataloging in Publication Data
Burchard, Marshall.   Sports Hero: Pete Rose.
(The Sports hero biographies)

   SUMMARY: A biography of the team captain of the
Cincinnati Reds, whose skills helped the team to
victory in the 1975 World Series, their first
championship in thirty-five years.
   1.   Rose, Pete, 1942—Juvenile literature.
2.   Baseball—Juvenile literature. [1. Rose,
Pete, 1942- 2.   Baseball—Biography]   I.   Title.
GV865.R65B87   796.357'092'4   [B]   [92]   76-25894
ISBN 0-399-20549-7
ISBN 0-399-61038-3 lib. bdg.

Contents

Pete Rose on the Western Hills High School
football team in 1959. He is number 55.

The Cincinnati Kid

Peter Edward Rose was born on April 14, 1942, in Cincinnati, Ohio. His family lived in a house on a hill overlooking the Ohio River, in a town just west of the city called Anderson Ferry. Pete was the third of four children. He had two older sisters, Jackie and Caryle, and a younger brother, David.

Pete's family was Irish. His father was named Harry Francis Rose, but everybody called him Pete. He liked the name and gave it to his first son. After that, Mr. Rose was known as Pete Senior or Big Pete. Pete was known as Pete Junior or Little Pete.

On weekdays Pete's father worked as a cashier in a bank. He found it boring work. Keeping track of all those numbers gave him headaches. On weekends he enjoyed playing sports. Depending on the season, Big Pete played baseball, football, or basketball. For a time he even boxed.

When Pete was born, Mr. Rose was glad to have a son he could teach to be an athlete.

"Daddy wanted a boy real bad," says Pete's older sister Jackie. "Daddy loved sports, and when Pete came along, he was tickled."

Pete and his father in 1971.

Pete learned to play hard by watching his father in action. Mr. Rose's best sport was football. He was a star halfback in a rugged league of semipro teams from Ohio and Kentucky. Pete was the water boy for his father's team.

"I'm the way I am because of my dad," Pete says. "He was a hustler, too, always running around and trying to win. If you tackled him high, he'd straight-arm you to death. If you tackled him low, he'd run right over you. He had more guts than any two guys I've ever known. He wasn't a dirty player either. He just wanted to win."

After the football games Mr. Rose was bruised and battered. But he always ran up the hill on his way home.

One game stands out in Pete's memory. It was the day he saw his father kick off, run down the field after the ballcarrier, and have his hip broken by a hard block. Instead of lying there waiting to be carried off on a stretcher, Mr. Rose tried to crawl along the ground and make the tackle.

"That was the kind of man he was," Pete says proudly.

As soon as Pete was old enough to walk, his father taught him to play catch. When Pete was strong enough to swing a bat, his father taught him how to hit.

Pete was naturally a right-handed batter. But Mr. Rose taught him to bat left-handed as well. Mr. Rose wanted his son to learn to be a switch-hitter. That way Pete could bat right-handed against left-handed pitchers and bat left-handed against right-handed pitchers. By switching from one side of the plate to the other, Pete could make sure that the curveballs were always breaking in toward his body instead of breaking out away from him. It's easier for a batter to hit curves that break in

Today Pete still swings the bat from both
sides of the plate.

toward him. Mr. Rose knew that by
teaching his son to switch-hit he would
be giving him an advantage.

"At first I wasn't too good left-handed," Pete says. "But Dad made me stay with it until I got good at it."

13

Mr. Rose often took Pete out to the ball park to watch the Cincinnati Reds. At home they followed the Reds' games on TV. One day they were watching the Reds play when Enos Slaughter of the St. Louis Cardinals drew a base on balls. Instead of trotting casually to first base the way most players do after walking, Slaughter dashed full tilt for the bag as though he were trying to beat out a hit. Pete was impressed by Slaughter's spirit.

"I decided right then that that was what I was going to do as long as I played ball," Pete says.

When he was nine, Pete began playing baseball in the Knot Hole League. His position was catcher.

Mr. Rose made the manager promise to let Pete be a switch-hitter, no matter what.

"He'll probably be weak left-handed," Mr. Rose told the manager. "But if you want Pete to play for you all summer, he's got to be a switcher."

Big Pete quit his own baseball team so that he could devote himself to his son's career.

"You're the athlete now," he told Pete.

When Pete was out on the field, his father was in the stands, urging him on. Even when Pete couldn't hear what Mr. Rose was saying, he could look over and read his lips. His dad's message was always the same:

"Hustle, Pete. Keep hustling."

Going for a touchdown in high school.

High School Shrimp

In his first year at Western Hills High School Pete went out for football. He played halfback and was captain of the freshman team. In the winter he played basketball. In the spring he played baseball.

Pete was tough, but he was short and weighed only about 130 pounds. The freshman baseball coach told him he wasn't big enough to be a catcher anymore. Pete switched to playing second base.

Mr. Rose followed his son's athletic career closely. After watching Pete play, his father often criticized his performance.

"It's funny but I used to feel sorry for Pete," says his sister Jackie. "He'd come home having done these terrific things in sports, and Daddy would concentrate only on the bad things he'd done. He never wanted Pete to get too self-satisfied, to get to the point where he wasn't always trying to do better."

In the fall of his second year in high school Pete hoped to play football for the varsity. But the coaches didn't want him on the team because they thought he was too small. Pete was bitterly disappointed.

"At that time," he says, "football

was a big thing to me, my dad being a football player and all. Well, I was little, but I was tough like my dad. But they said I was too small. That hurt me, hurt me real bad. You can imagine how my dad felt.''

Pete lost interest in school. He cut classes and got into fights. His thoughts all ran to sports. As a result, he flunked and had to repeat his sophomore year.

After that Pete did better in school. He grew just enough bigger for the coaches to let him play varsity football. He was still a shrimp compared to most of the other players. But his hard running helped the team upset their main rival, Elder High, and finish in a tie for first place in the local high school championship.

Pete played second base for the varsity baseball team. As a fielder he was no better than all right. But he was a skillful hitter, and though he wasn't terribly speedy, he hustled harder than anybody else on the team.

During the summers he played sandlot baseball. His parents never asked him to take a summer job. His father didn't want anything to interfere with Pete's play.

"Sports was his only job growing up," Pete's father said later, "but he did the job right."

Because he had to repeat a grade, it took Pete five years to finish high school. According to the rules, he could play only four years of high school sports. So instead of playing baseball for Western Hills his senior year, he played for a team from Lebanon, Ohio, that competed in the Dayton Amateur League. Lebanon was thirty miles away. Pete didn't have a car but he always managed to find a ride. His batting average that spring was a hot .500.

During his senior year Pete was invited by the Cincinnati Reds to work out with other promising youngsters from the area at Crosley Field, the Reds' home ball park. He got to wear a Reds uniform and chase fly balls hit by some of his heroes on afternoons when the Cincinnati players took batting practice.

The first afternoon Pete practiced with the Reds his father hurried to the ball park as soon as he finished working at the bank. When Mr. Rose saw Pete out on the field wearing a Cincinnati uniform, he was so proud and happy he cried.

When Pete graduated from high school, there were two big-league scouts who thought he was promising enough to play professional baseball. One of them worked for the Baltimore Orioles. The other one worked for the Cincinnati Reds.

The Cincinnati scout, Buddy Bloebaum, was Pete's uncle. Bloebaum naturally wanted his nephew to sign with

A slide into base
for the Western Hills team.

the Reds, but the men who ran the team weren't too impressed with Pete's prospects. He was still small, he didn't hit the ball with real power, and he didn't show great talent as a fielder.

Uncle Buddy set about convincing his bosses that Pete deserved a chance. Bloebaum told them the men in the Rose family were slow reaching their full size. He promised that Pete would soon be putting on more weight. He told them about how hard Pete hustled and how much he wanted to play for his hometown team.

Buddy Bloebaum kept talking until the Reds agreed to offer Pete a deal. Shortly after his graduation Pete signed a $7,000 contract to play Class D Pony League baseball for a Cincinnati farm team in Geneva, New York.

Life in the Minors

Pete was eighteen when he went off to the small town of Geneva, New York, to begin his career as a professional ballplayer. It was the first time he had ever lived away from home. He moved into a rooming house with three other players, but despite their company, he was lonely and missed his family and friends back home.

His father wrote to him often. At the

end of his letters Mr. Rose always printed the same advice in large capital letters: "KEEP ON WINNING. KEEP HUSTLING. KEEP WORKING HARD."

Playing second base for Geneva, Pete appeared in 85 games. His batting average was only .277, and he led the league in errors with 36.

Pete slides headfirst into third base.

That winter Pete did some growing. He took a job back home in Cincinnati loading boxcars. It was heavy work and helped develop his muscles.

"I weighed about a hundred and sixty when I started," he says. "I began to gain weight and kept right on gaining until I reached a hundred ninety-five pounds."

The next summer Pete moved up to another Cincinnati farm team in Tampa, Florida. He raised his batting average to .331 and led the league in hitting triples with 30.

His 30 triples was a new team record. The day he set it his parents were there to watch. After Pete hit the triple that broke the record he called time-out, got the ball back, and ran over to the stands to give it to his mother.

The following year Pete moved another notch higher in the Reds' farm system. He spent the summer of 1962 playing for Macon, Georgia.

As he made his way up through the minor leagues, Pete was the talk of all the players because of the way he always hustled. A lot of players thought he was just showing off. They called him Hotdog and Hollywood.

"They couldn't believe he was for real," says Pete's Cincinnati teammate Jack Billingham, who played against him in Florida. "They'd talk about him on buses. I'd hear all about this kid who runs out walks and never stops talking."

At first the manager at Macon, Dave Bristol, didn't know what to make of Pete.

Hustlin' Pete Rose.

"The first time I saw Rose I kind of sat back and watched him running all the time to everywhere. I asked myself, 'Is he putting me on with all this razzmatazz, or is he real? Is it going to be like this all the time?' Well, it was! He never gave up all year—not once on anything."

Going for home plate.

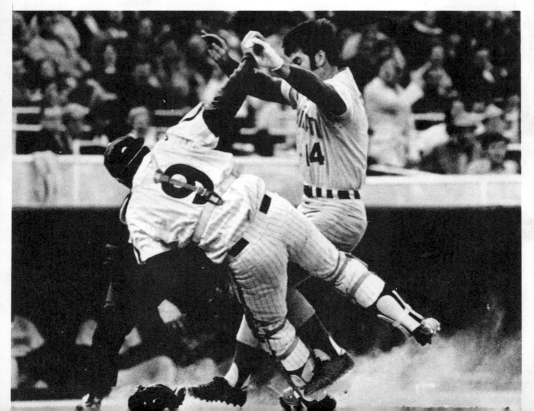

To keep everybody loose, Pete liked to play a joke now and then. Manager Bristol remembers one that Pete played on the Macon catcher, Larry Himes.

"Himes was having his troubles throwing. His throws would go over the heads of Rose and Tommy Helms at second base and wind up in center field. All the time Himes would be yelling at Rose and Helms, 'Pick me up, you gotta pick me up!'

"One day I came out to the park and Himes was catching batting practice, and there were Rose and Helms on second base. They had a stepladder, and Rose was on the top of it and Helms halfway up, and they were hollering, 'Pick us up, Larry, pick us up!' "

Another time Pete decided to scare the wits out of his teammate Art Shamsky. It was late at night, and a bunch of players were traveling down the highway in a station wagon. Shamsky was driving. While the others dozed, Pete quietly crawled out the back window and up onto the roof. As the ground around him sped by at sixty miles an hour, he pulled himself forward until he reached the front windshield.

Shamsky suddenly saw a hand reaching down right in front of him on the other side of the glass. He was so startled he almost drove off the road. The other players woke up to see the upside-down face of Pete Rose grinning in at them through the windshield.

Pete had a good year at Macon. He batted .330 and led the league in triples and runs scored.

After the end of his third year in the minors the Reds decided it was time to give him a shot at the big leagues. In 1963 they invited him to their spring training camp in Florida.

Riverfront Stadium: Home of the Cincinnati
Reds.

Rookie Year

Pete was twenty-one when he went to Tampa in March, 1963, for his first spring training with the Reds. He was determined to win a spot on the club, but hardly anybody thought he could do it. The one Cincinnati player who did think Pete might make it was second baseman Don Blasingame, the man whose job Pete was out to take. Everybody else expected that the Reds would cut Pete from the squad and send him to their top farm team in San Diego, California, for one more year of minor-league seasoning.

Pete got a chance to show what he could do during Cincinnati's first exhibition game of the spring against the Chicago White Sox. He wasn't supposed to be in the lineup that day. But he hung around the dugout anyway, hoping that the Cincinnati manager, Fred Hutchinson, would notice him and put him into the game.

The game was a scoreless tie. When it went into extra innings, Hutchinson began running out of players. Seeing Pete, he put him in at second base. In the eleventh inning Pete lashed a double. In the fourteenth he hit another double and then came home with the game-winning run.

As spring training went on, Pete built his reputation for being a man who tried his hardest on every play. He ran to and from his position, he ran to first after walks, and he usually slid into bases headfirst on his belly in a cloud of dust.

Sliding into third with a triple against the Braves.

One day the Reds were playing an exhibition game against the New York Yankees. Before the game the Yankee stars Whitey Ford and Mickey Mantle watched Pete run around in practice.

"What's that thing supposed to be?" asked Ford.

"One of the funniest things I ever saw," said Mantle.

Pete jumps in the air to grab a wild pickoff throw at second base.

"I've got a name for that thing," said Ford. "That's Charlie Hustle."

Pete never doubted he would make the Reds. One night after practice Coach Dick Sisler saw him walking along the highway from the Tampa ball park to the team motel. Pete had stayed so late after practice he'd missed the team bus. Sisler wanted to know how come he was walking.

"Well," said Pete, "I didn't have cab fare, and you wouldn't expect a major leaguer to hitchhike, would you?"

Pete's confidence in himself turned out to be well justified. He not only made the Reds, but he beat out veteran Don Blasingame for the job of starting second baseman.

Cincinnati opened the 1963 season

with a home game against the Pittsburgh Pirates. Pete's whole family and a lot of his friends were there to root for him.

Pete was the leadoff hitter. The first time he came to bat he drew a walk on four straight pitches. When he ran to first, the crowd cheered. Frank Robinson came to bat and homered, driving Pete in with the first run of the season.

Pete went hitless that day. He let one ball go through his legs for an error, but he also helped make four double plays. After the game, which was won by Cincinnati, he was smiling.

The next day Pete batted against the Pirates' Bob Friend, one of the league's best pitchers. Pete lined a hit into left field and tried to stretch it into a triple. While the fielders chased the ball, he rounded second base without stopping and barreled on toward third. As the throw came in from the outfield, he dived on his belly and slid headfirst into the bag. He was safe with his first major-league hit.

Diving into third.

During the first part of the season Pete had his troubles. Against the Philadelphia Phillies one day he struck out four straight times.

Most of the veteran Cincinnati players were giving him the cold shoulder. They thought he was a show-off, and they didn't like him for beating their friend Don Blasingame out of his job.

"The team was cliquey," says Pete, "and the white guys for the most part wouldn't have anything to do with me. I hung around with the blacks. Frank Robinson and Vada Pinson helped me tremendously."

As the season continued, the rest of the Reds gradually began to accept Pete as a member of the team. His play improved, especially at the plate, and he wound up the year with 170 hits and a batting average of .273. The Reds came in fifth.

Of Pete's rookie year Frank Robinson says, "It wasn't apparent to anyone that he had the kind of ability he turned out to have. You could see he had hustle, desire, and drive, and

At a lunch counter with teammate Frank Robinson.

Pete and Karolyn at their wedding.

you knew he'd get a lot of hits because he'd leg 'em out, but no one could foresee him leading the league."

One day when the Reds weren't playing, Pete spent the afternoon at the racetrack. Looking through his binoculars, he noticed a girl standing near the rail. He liked the way she looked and arranged to be introduced. Her name was Karolyn Englehardt.

Pete married Karolyn in January, 1964, in the off-season following his rookie year. He was several hours late for the wedding reception. While the guests waited, Pete was off accepting the award as the National League's Rookie of the Year.

All-Star at Twenty-three

In 1964, in his second year in the majors, Pete fell victim to the sophomore slump. When the season was two months old, he was batting barely .200. He worried about ending the slump and took advice from Manager Fred Hutchinson and Batting Coach Ted Kluszewski.

Pete tried all kinds of changes in his batting style. Nothing worked. Finally, one day Hutchinson called him into his office.

"Pete," said Hutch, "I know you've been trying what we wanted you to do, but it doesn't seem to be working. Go back the way you were doing it."

In the middle of that season, illness forced Hutch to give up his managing job. Dick Sisler was named the new manager.

One day in Houston, Sisler benched Pete for showing poor judgment at the plate. At the next team practice the manager asked Pete to field some grounders at third base, and Pete refused.

"He told me he wouldn't play third," Sisler told a reporter. "I called him up to the hotel room afterward and chewed him out pretty good."

"It was a misunderstanding," Pete said. "I thought they were giving up on me completely, and it teed me off. I wanted to play second base."

After the talk with Sisler, Pete was more cooperative. The next day he not only fielded grounders at third, but also put on pads and volunteered to catch batting practice.

Pete tossing the ball in practice.

Hammering out a hit.

Soon Pete was back on the job at second base. He continued to have trouble at the plate. Sometimes he was hot, but often he was not. He finished the year with only 139 hits and a batting average of .269.

If Pete had come through with more hits, the Reds might have wound up playing in the World Series. As it was, they missed coming in first in their division by one game.

When the season was over, the Reds told Pete he needed to work on improving his fielding. He had trouble with balls hit to his right, and he wasn't smooth enough in making double plays. When he took the throw from the shortstop and stepped on second for out number one, he drew back his arm for the relay to first instead of flipping the ball in one lightning catch-and-throw motion.

The Reds urged him to go to Venezuela during the off-season and play winter ball with the Caracas Lions. The manager was a Cincinnati coach named Reggie Otero, who would help Pete work on his fielding.

The Lions played three games a

week. On the other four days Otero made Pete practice playing second base. He had him spend hours fielding grounders and practicing the double play.

"Baseball players are like ballerinas," says Otero. "They must practice until their feet are sore and then practice some more."

Otero wore Rose out.

"If Pete was a different kind of kid, he would have told me to go to hell," Otero says. "He would get so tired he'd fall down. I'd tell him to rest five minutes, and then we'd go at it some more."

One day in the dugout during a game Pete got mad at Otero. For losing his temper Otero fined him 500 bolivars, the equivalent in Venezuelan money of 150 U.S. dollars.

"Look," Otero told him, "you going to make big money next year and it ain't for me. It's for Pete Rose."

While Pete was in South America, he was saddened by the news of Fred Hutchinson's death.

"Hutch treated me like a man," said Pete. "He tried to help me like a father. He was an exceptional person."

Pete spent all winter playing for Caracas. He led the league in runs scored and improved his play at second base. In the spring he headed for Florida to join the rest of the Reds as they prepared for the start of the 1965 season. Pete could hardly wait for opening day.

It turned out to be a poor year for the team. The Reds finished in fourth place. But it was a great year for Pete.

He played in all 162 games. He had 670 at bats, which was more than any

Seven members of the Cincinnati Reds were named to the 1965 National League All-Star team. Left to right are shortstop Leo Cardenas, catcher John Edwards, right fielder Frank Robinson, manager Dick Sisler, pitchers Jim Maloney and Sammy Ellis, and second baseman Pete Rose.

other National League player, and he led the league in hits with 209. He was third in the league in doubles with 35 and third in runs scored with 117. His batting average of .312 was the league's fifth highest.

Pete was named to the National League All-Star team. At twenty-three, after three seasons in the majors, he was looking forward to a great career.

Captain Pete

As the years passed, Pete built a reputation not only as a great hitter, but also as the game's top hustler. Nobody outhustled him because he wasn't about to let it happen.

"I give a hundred and ten per cent," he said. "I don't just give a hundred per cent because some guy opposite me might be giving that much. If you have a guy equal in ability to me, I'm gonna beat him because I'll try harder. That guy ain't got a chance.''

In 1967 Pete was switched from the infield to the outfield. At first he played in right. Later he moved over to left. His hard charging and strong throwing made him one of the league's best outfielders.

Nowhere was Pete's fiery spirit clearer than when he ran the bases. Though he lacked the speed to be a great base stealer, his daring running often let him take an extra base, stretching a single into a double or a double into a triple. He fought hard to get on base, and once on, he fought hard to get around and score. His hallmark on the base paths was the belly-whopping headfirst slide.

Pete slid headfirst because he believed it was easier, faster, and safer than the usual feetfirst slide.

"You actually gain momentum," he said. "You land on your arms. Maybe it hurts more, but what's hurting anyway? You can break your ankle or your leg a lot faster than you can break your belly or your arm. And I don't want to miss any games. And besides, you usually get your picture in the paper, too."

A number of times Pete even slid headfirst into home plate. It was not something he recommended to others.

"You can wind up getting cut to pieces by the catcher's shinguards," he said. "It's happened to me more than once."

Instead of sliding into home plate, Pete learned to keep his feet. When a

Trying to score, Pete slams hard into Los
Angeles Dodgers catcher Duke Sims, hoping
to make him drop the ball.

catcher blocked his way, Pete lowered
his shoulder like a halfback and
crashed right into him. Often the im-
pact jarred the ball loose from the
catcher's hand, enabling Pete to score.

Sims recoils but holds onto the ball and Rose
is out.

Pete gave a lot of the credit for his
success in the big leagues to his tough
5-foot-11 inch, 200-pound body.

"I'm built strong and stocky like my
dad," he said. "I'm always in perfect

shape. I may lose ten pounds during a sunny doubleheader, but I'll go out and eat a steak and salad and put it back. And I don't smoke. Or drink much, a cold beer now and then.''

Pete's body served him well. Considering his aggressive style of play, he picked up relatively few injuries. When he was hurt, he didn't let it keep him out of the lineup for long.

In 1968, he was injured on the second day of the season. Playing in the outfield, he leaped up to try to save a home run and ripped his hand open on a wire fence. The next day he appeared at the ball park with his hand bandaged shut, got two hits, and started a streak in which he hit safely in 22 straight games.

Later that season he broke his thumb

Climbing the fence to save a home run.

trying for a diving catch. In the locker room he asked the doctor how long he'd have to be out of action.

"An injury like this should keep most athletes out five or six weeks," said the doctor. "But knowing you, I'd say about three weeks."

The very next day Pete suited up and got into the game as a pinch runner. Exactly three weeks later, just as the doctor predicted, he was back playing regularly again.

Despite missing those three weeks, Pete still managed to make 210 hits. He led the major leagues in batting with an average of .335. He committed only three errors all year and, thanks to good throwing, led all National League outfielders in assists with 20.

"I wanted that," said Pete of his leadership in assists. "I cut off a lot of runs at home plate."

The National League award for Most Valuable Player of 1968 went to pitcher Bob Gibson of the St. Louis Cardinals. Pete disagreed with the choice.

"I think I should have gotten the award," he said. "I don't believe a pitcher should be judged on the same basis as an everyday player. Gibson's a heck of a pitcher, and he had a heck of a year, but he was in thirty-four games and I was in one hundred and forty-nine. He won twenty-two games for the Cards. I might have won fifty for the Reds.''

In 1969 Pete cracked out 218 hits and won his second straight batting crown with an average of .348. He was again outvoted for the Most Valuable Player award, but his performance earned him another goal he had been seeking. He became the first baseball player not a home run hitter or 20-game-winning pitcher to receive a salary of $100,000 a year.

''Usually players prefer to keep their salaries secret,'' he said, ''but I want the whole world to know about this.''

In 1970 Sparky Anderson took over as the Reds' manager. Pete offered to

Rose and manager Sparky Anderson at
spring training.

help his new boss any way he could.

"I make the most money on this
team," Pete told Sparky. "I'll do anything you want."

Sparky made Pete the team captain.
Pete set out to lead the Reds to the
pennant. Cincinnati had a new ball
park, Riverfront Stadium, and the
Reds hoped to celebrate its opening by
winning their first championship in
many a moon.

During the year Pete's brother
Dave came home from Vietnam. The

whole Rose family rejoiced at Dave's safe return from the war.

The Reds won the National League pennant for the first time since Pete had joined the team. But they lost the World Series to the American League champion Baltimore Orioles.

That winter Pete's father came home from work early one day feeling sick. As he walked in the door, he dropped dead of a heart attack. He was fifty-eight.

Pete took his father's death hard, but he learned to accept it.

"When you lose somebody you're close to, you can cry all you want," Pete said. "But my dad got to see me win batting titles, play in All-Star games and in the World Series. The way I look at it, I repaid him."

Rose upends Chicago shortstop Don Kessinger to break up a double play.

World Champions

In 1972 the Reds strengthened their team with a trade. They got second baseman Joe Morgan and pitcher Jack Billingham from Houston. Morgan and Rose became good friends. Joe was in awe of the way Pete hustled.

"When I played against him," said Joe, "I assumed nobody went that hard all the time, that he did that just against us. Now that I have seen him day in and day out, I find him amazing."

Billingham was impressed by Rose, too.

"Pete might go oh for four," Billingham said, "but if we'd win the game, he'd be the happiest guy in the clubhouse. You notice things like that."

"It's all a matter of wanting to win," said Pete. "Winning is the only thing."

In 1973 Pete won his third batting crown and led the Reds to another pennant. He was finally named the National League's Most Valuable Player of the Year.

During the 1973 National League play-offs against New York, Pete was trying to break up a double play when he barreled hard into the Mets' shortstop, Bud Harrelson, who was covering second base. Harrelson was mad.

With the dust from the slide still in the air,
Rose and Harrelson start fighting.

He said something to Rose, and Rose
said something back. Suddenly they
were fighting.

After they were separated, the Mets

fans booed and shouted insults at Rose. When he took the field the following day, they greeted him with a barrage of garbage and bottles. It was an unpleasant sort of reception, to say the least, and as it turned out, Pete had to get used to it. The idea proved catching, and the following season fans in other cities welcomed him to their ball parks with similar bombardments and abuse.

Mets fan holds up a sign as Pete trots to the dugout.

The Reds beat the Mets in the 1973 play-offs and won the National League pennant. For the second time in Pete's career the Reds made it into the World Series, and for the second time they lost, this time to the Oakland Athletics.

Cincinnati's third crack at the World Series came two years later in 1975. Early in the season the Reds had trouble scoring runs because their big sluggers, Johnny Bench and Tony Perez, weren't hitting. To get more punch into the attack, Sparky Anderson asked Pete to switch from left field to third base so that the Reds could put the heavy-hitting George Foster in the line-up in left field.

Pete hadn't played in the infield for eight years. Back in 1966 the Reds had tried switching him from second to third base and he had balked at the idea, playing only 16 games at the position. He had been in the outfield ever since.

This time, when Anderson asked him to play third base, Pete readily agreed. He was taking a risk moving to an unfamiliar position, but he was willing to do anything that might help the team.

With his usual zeal Pete didn't just go through the motions of playing his new position; he set out to master it. He worked so hard perfecting his fielding that he set an example for the whole team to follow.

"He's an inspiration to our younger players," said Batting Coach Ted Kluszewski. "They see him out there busting his butt and they say, 'Hey, maybe this is how it's done up here.'"

Ripping a single up the middle.

With Rose at third and Foster in left the Reds started to roll. They scored their runs in bunches and won their games in streaks. No matter how many runs they might be behind, they never stopped trying to win. Again and again when they were trailing, they put on big rallies in the late innings to come from behind.

One day they were taking a beating from the St. Louis Cardinals. When Pete came to bat in the eighth inning, his team was down seven runs, there were two out, and the bases were empty. Pete beat out an infield hit and started the Reds off on an eight-run rally that won the game.

"You never know what's gonna happen in a baseball game," he said.

The Reds breezed home with the pennant. Then they played the Boston Red Sox in the World Series.

The October showdown between the two major league champions was one of the most exciting and hardest-fought World Series ever played. It was a contest of comebacks, and the lead changed back and forth. Boston won the first game. The Reds tied it up.

Boston's Dwight Evans reaching third base
with a triple in game four.

Boston won again. The Reds tied it up
again. The Reds won again and moved
into the lead.

Then came game six. As Pete looks
back on his long career in the major
leagues, he calls game six, a dramatic
come-from-behind victory for the Red
Sox, the most exciting game he's ever

played in. Though Cincinnati lost game six, Pete was anything but glum in the locker room later.

"What a ball game!" he told reporters. "I'm proud just to have participated. If this ain't the number one sport, what is?"

In the deciding game seven, the Red Sox took a 3–0 lead. In the sixth inning Pete slid into second base so hard he

Red Sox catcher Carlton Fisk tags Rose out at home plate in game five.

Pete gives himself a hand after
diving safely into third base
in the final game.

broke up a double play that would have
ended the inning. Tony Perez followed
with a two-run homer, and the Reds
narrowed the score to 3–2.

When Cincinnati took the field again,
Pete went to work stirring up the team.
He bounced around at his position,
pounded his glove, and shouted encour-
agements. His will to win at that mo-
ment was so strong that even people in

the stands felt it. It turned on the whole Cincinnati team. They were still behind one run, but they were so charged up that their ultimate victory seemed certain. When it came, it was Pete who drove in the tying run, and Joe Morgan who drove in the winner.

It was the first time Cincinnati had won the World Series since 1940. The whole town went wild over the victory. Pete was proud that the part he'd played in it earned him the award as Most Valuable Player of the Series.

Said Pete, ''What gives me the most pleasure in this game is just seeing people's faces, seeing how excited they get about us winning the World Series, having people come up to me saying, 'Thanks.' That's what this is all about.''

After the excitement was all over, he still couldn't stop thinking about baseball.

"I wish next season was starting tomorrow," he said.

A Feeling for Winning

Of all his personal accomplishments as a major-league ballplayer, Pete is proudest of the number of seasons he's been able to make 200 or more hits. Making 200 hits in a season is one of the most difficult goals a batter can achieve. The Sultan of Swat himself, Babe Ruth, managed to do it only three times. Joe DiMaggio did it only twice, Willie Mays did it only once, and Ted

Receiving the 1974 Most Valuable Player
award from Warren Giles, former president of
the National League.

Williams and Mickey Mantle never did
it at all.

After thirteen years in the majors,
Pete has done it seven times. He is
closing in on the big-league record of
nine 200-hit seasons, set by Ty Cobb
back in the 1920s.

Pete's record makes him a sure bet
for the Baseball Hall of Fame. In his
thirteen seasons he has batted .300 or

higher ten times, scored 100 or more runs eight times, won three batting championships (1968, 1969, and 1973) and racked up 2,547 hits, as well as won two Gold Gloves for his fielding. His goal is to make 3,000 hits before he quits.

At the plate Pete tries to bat for a high average. He hits lots of singles, doubles, and triples, but few home runs. The most he's hit in any one season is 16.

"I never think home run when I get up there," he says. "I just think 'Hit the ball hard.' "

Instead of swinging for the fences, Pete tries to line out hits. He is proud of his ability to make base hits and thinks there's too much emphasis on home runs.

Hitting a single to left field.

"Sure a home run may be worth four singles," he says. "But if the home run hitter strikes out his next three times up, while the singles hitter gets four hits, that's four runs his team may score instead of one. Managers have to think of this more."

At bat Pete crouches over the plate, protecting the strike zone. When he swings, he tries to keep his bat level. He swings hard, but he doesn't try to overpower the ball. By holding just a little back, he gains greater control of his bat and a better chance of making contact with the ball.

"Make contact," he says, "and you've always got a chance for a hit."

Like most skillful batters, Pete hits the ball where it's pitched. This means that if a ball is pitched in tight to him, he tries to hit it to the near field, while if it's pitched outside, he tries to hit it to the far field. Whenever possible he likes to hit it up the middle because that's where the biggest opening is.

"It doesn't look big when you're at the plate because you've got the pitcher standing in front of you," he says. "But if you hit the ball right back at him, the chances are it'll get past him because he usually won't be quick enough to pick off a hard-hit ball at that distance."

Pete bears down hard each time he comes to bat. No matter how many hits he may have made in a game, he always tries for more.

"A writer once told me Stan Musial went after a hit his first trip up, then another and another," Pete says. "That's my system, too. As many hits as I can get."

Pitchers are Pete's enemy. His opinion of most of them is low.

"I don't think enough of 'em are good athletes," he says. "They can't hit, can't field, can't bunt, can't run. I wouldn't want a job where I played only once every fifth day."

He admits to respecting a few top pitchers like Tom Seaver and Jon Matlack of the New York Mets and Don Sutton of the Los Angeles Dodgers.

"But," says Pete, "none of 'em really give me any trouble—I can hit 'em all."

"Confidence is the big thing that makes Rose a great hitter," says home run king Hank Aaron. "Rose believes that there isn't anybody who can get him out."

"I want to be thought of as one of the best players Cincinnati ever had," Pete says. And so he is. His performance over the years has earned him the respect of players and coaches throughout baseball. Even the men with whom he has tangled admit to liking him.

"He is probably one of the best all-around batting and fielding players in the majors," says his 1973 play-off foe, Bud Harrelson of the Mets. "I had that run-in with Pete, but I sure admire the guy."

Rival manager Gene Mauch calls Pete the kind of ballplayer every manager likes to manage. Says Mauch, "He's proud of being the game's top

Even in spring training, Pete gives it all he's got.

hustler, and he goes out to try to prove every day that his reputation is justified."

When he's playing, Pete spends all the energy he has.

"I never admit I'm tired," he says. "When other guys are slowing down, I'm coming on."

Off the field he likes to save up his strength. When he travels to other cities with the team, he doesn't spend his time out on the town. Usually, he doesn't even leave his hotel.

"I just stay in my room and watch TV," he says. "When I first started playing, I liked to go see the Statue of Liberty and Fisherman's Wharf and all those things, but once you've seen 'em you've seen 'em. So I just watch TV.

Surrounded by trophies, Rose shows his son Pete a check for more than $19,000, his share for winning the 1975 World Series.

New York and LA are my favorite cities to visit because they've got all-night movies on TV."

Today Pete earns almost $200,000 a year playing baseball. That is as much as the President of .the United States earns for running the country.

"Everybody tries to make what they're worth," Pete says. "I don't play for the buck only, but it is an important part of it. No amount of extra money could make me play any harder than I do. But I do want to be paid for playing hard."

When his playing days are through, Pete plans to become a manager.

"I have this feeling for winning," he says. "When my legs go, my desire will still be high. Managing is a way to stay close to the game for a while. I think I'd be good at it."

When people start comparing Pete to other baseball greats, they often mention players like Roberto Clemente, Lou Brock, Enos Slaughter, and the legendary Georgia Peach, Ty Cobb. The comparisons are flattering, but none of them suits Pete quite right.

"He's an original," says Reds coach Kluszewski. "You won't see another like him for a thousand years."

"I wish I could always be around people like Pete," says Manager Sparky Anderson. "He'll never think old. Energywise, he'll always be eighteen."

About the Author

Marshall Burchard, a writer and sports fan, lives on the East Coast.

He has recently written Sports Hero biographies of Muhammad Ali, Reggie Jackson, Dr. J., Jimmy Connors, and Fred Lynn.

He has been the coauthor of numerous other Sports Hero biographies, among them *Joe Namath, Brooks Robinson, Bobby Orr, Roger Staubach, Larry Csonka, Billie Jean King, O. J. Simpson, Phil Esposito,* and *Richard Petty.*